BRILLIANT
LIVING

31 INSIGHTS TO CREATING AN
AWESOME LIFE

SIMON T. BAILEY

SOUND WISDOM

P.O. Box 310

Shippensburg, PA 17257-0310

For more information on publishing and distribution rights, call 717-530-2122 or info@soundwisdom.com.

Quantity Sales. Special discounts are available on quantity purchases by corporations, associations, and others. For details, contact the Sales Department at Sound Wisdom.

While efforts have been made to verify information contained in this publication, neither the author nor the publisher assumes any responsibility for errors, inaccuracies, or omissions.

While this publication is chock-full of useful, practical information, it is not intended to be legal or accounting advice. All readers are advised to seek competent lawyers and accountants to follow laws and regulations that may apply to specific situations.

The reader of this publication assumes responsibility for the use of the information. The author and publisher assume no responsibility or liability whatsoever on behalf of the reader of this publication.

ISBN 13 TP: 978-1-937879-73-0

ISBN 13 Ebook: 978-0-7684-1136-2

For Worldwide Distribution, Printed in the U.S.A.

3 4 5 6 7 8 / 19 18 17

Credits:

Editor Nancy Baumann, The Book Professor, St. Louis, MO

Contributing Editor: Bevrlee Lips, Orlando, FL

Carolyn Bartholomew, Nashville, TN

Melissa Spencer, Orlando, FL

Jessica Vick, Orlando, FL

Kathleen Green, Positively Proofed

Cover/Jacket designer Eileen Rockwell

Interior design by Terry Clifton

DEDICATION

This book is dedicated to all people who are pursuing meaning over money, purpose instead of power, and significance instead of success. We need you. The world needs you. And the future awaits you, O' Brilliant One.

INTRODUCTION

O' Brilliant One,

Are you tired of waiting, concerned about where things are going? Or are you simply ready to shift your life, career, or business into high gear? If so, you're ready for brilliant living.

This inspirational guide will help you do just that, to experience the amazing effects and reap the untold rewards of living a brilliant life.

I believe that there are eight core areas of life that we must constantly evaluate to live a brilliant life: spiritual, family, career/business, emotional, mental, wellness, social, and financial. Each of these lessons can be used to enhance one specific core area or several of them at the same time.

I believe that when you intentionally analyze and attend to these core areas, you will significantly improve your life.

For the next thirty-one days, carve out fifteen minutes every morning for this meditation routine, which is chunked into five-minute increments. Use the first five minutes to read an inspirational message from this book. Begin the second five minutes by taking two or three deep breaths and letting them out slowly. Then practice complete silence for the entire five minutes.

Take the last five minutes to stand up and stretch your arms and legs. This daily commitment realigns your head, heart, and hands and breathes life into you so that no matter what headwinds of change come your way, you can face it. These are some of the insights I learned throughout my career while working at Disney, mentoring emerging leaders, and coaching hundreds of professionals in for-profit and non-profit organizations.

These readings provide inspiration and practical steps that, when applied, will help you move from being an average performer to becoming a brilliant producer. I encourage you to read them first thing in the morning when your mind is clear, but if you are an evening person, it can also work if you read them just before you fall asleep.

Affirm each Brilliant Decree out loud, and be sure to do the work of each Brilliant Next Step by writing it down in your journal. Affirmation (Brilliant Decree) + Application (Brilliant Next Step) = Your Results.

At the end of the month, repeat the process and reread each lesson over the next two months. Why? Because every season lasts about three months, and your life recycles and starts anew every ninety days. In fact, ninety percent of your blood cells are reborn every three months.

Reach out to an accountability partner and share these daily inspirations with them. Tell them what you have committed to work on every day.

Share these lessons with your teenage children and on social media. Tweet them with the hashtag #BrilliantLiving31, post them on Facebook, put them on Pinterest, LinkedIn, Vine, or whatever best works for you.

As a result of reading, affirming, and acting on a daily basis, I'm confident that you will be launched into brilliant living, where you will create your own tomorrows, not just warmed-over versions of today, but entirely new, exciting, history-making moments.

Enjoy this journey to leading, loving, and brilliant living!

Simon T. Bailey

INSIGHT 1
DARE TO BE BRILLIANT

(Family)

I was extremely blessed to have had a happy childhood, chock-full of great memories. When I reflect on my early life, what stirs up my inner "happy" the most are the simple times of childhood games and play. Hide-and-go-seek, tag, Simon Says (had to throw that in!), kickball—I loved them all.

Being the adventurer that I am, what I loved most was a good dare! Nothing got me more excited than a buddy screaming, "I dare you," or even more powerful, "I double-dog dare you!" I was wise even back then and never took on foolish dares, but otherwise, I never passed an opportunity to push past the limits to show someone what I could do. So, here goes:

I DARE YOU TO BE BRILLIANT!!

Welcome to the New Normal. This is a time in history when the people who take their timid feet off the brakes of life will accelerate into the future. I have news for you. The good old days may be behind us, but there are magnificent days just around the corner. Enough waiting around; enough biting your nails; enough tapping your feet, enough wishing and waiting for something to happen. Consider this your nudge, your push, your show.

Now is the time to take everything you do to the next dimension. Be brilliant. Average people show up. Brilliant people make a difference. Average people wait for something to happen. Brilliant people make things happen. Average people play it safe. Brilliant people take risks. Which one are you? Will you dare to be brilliant?

BRILLIANT DECREE

I dedicate myself to displaying my unique brilliance every day. The fruit of tomorrow lies in the seeds of today. Today I will plant seeds of brilliance through my actions, my speech, and my thoughts, in order to yield a vast harvest tomorrow.

BRILLIANT NEXT STEP

o Create a long-term strategic life plan that will positively impact your family and the next generation.

o Your plan should consider the eight core areas of your life—Spiritual, Family, Mental, Social, Wellness, Career/Business, Emotional, and Financial. Record how you intend to grow, develop, and add value.

o Break it down into a ninety-day plan, a one-year plan, a two-year plan, and a three-year plan. Share your plan with your spouse, best friend, or family member, and ask them to hold you accountable.

INSIGHT 2
TRANSITION—UNLEASH THE POWER OF METACONNECTION

(Mental)

Maybe it's time for you to make a move. You wake in the wee hours and wonder who is knocking at the door of your heart, then realize that the knocking is coming from inside.

Or perhaps the conversations you have with other people, conversations that you once enjoyed, now seem so elementary, so empty and bland. You don't want to be rude, but in the midst of such conversations, you completely check out. You hear what's being said but no longer connect with it.

Or you could be at the point of extreme dissatisfaction, distaste, or even disgust with the status quo. What once engaged you no longer interests or fulfills you.

Well, my friend, you've begun the process of transition. It's the point where your mind and heart intersect with your destiny, and you know it's time to step into the next dimension.

In this season of transition, you are getting ready to move to a place of metaconnection. Metaconnection is the state of mind when you are fully present, fully aligned, fully alive, and fully dialed in.

Metaconnection allows you to listen between the sentences. You release your need to be right and, instead, tune into the diverse thinking around you. You invite others to share their points of view, so that, together, you can reach the best solutions.

Brace yourself. You are getting ready to go where no man or woman has ever gone. This transition is going to take you beyond the familiar, past what's comfortable, and into what is totally strange. You will feel out of place, uncomfortable, and way beyond what is normal.

Here's the difference: You will stop pushing your way into the future. Instead, you will learn the art of pulling the future toward you.

Here are three things you can do while in the midst of transition:

1. **Listen** for the still, small voice of God within your heart that is directing you and telling you where to go next. That voice may not tell you what you want to hear, but it will be the exact thing that you need to do.

2. **Let go** of one-sided, needy, hooked-on-drama types of people who always take but never give. Don't worry about being liked or fitting in with the crowd, and stop chasing people so they'll be your friends. Don't call them, don't text them, and don't e-mail them. You're going to a rare place, and they cannot soar with you.

3. **Be curious.** Not everything that looks good is good, and anything that seems odd should be

questioned. Ask "why" questions. The moment you ask, you are primed to discover the answer that is waiting to come forth. The answers will not emerge until the questions have been asked.

A curious person is a thinking person. A curious person looks for what has not yet occurred, for what is waiting to emerge, rather than what has always been.

BRILLIANT DECREE

I am open to what wants
to emerge in my life.
I think clearly.
I am learning how to be totally
present in the moment and to pay
attention to everything around me.
I am letting go of performance-
based relationships that take
from me and never give.
I am listening with my ears and with
my heart. I am a careful observer of
everything that happens around me.

BRILLIANT
NEXT STEP

Read one book a month that stretches you. Create a summary of key takeaways from the book and share it with your family and friends to discover what questions they may have about it. When you share what you've learned with someone else, you learn it twice because the key takeaways become anchored in you.

YOU ARE THE BRILLIANT
PIECE TO THE PUZZLE

Spiritual

Did you ever work jigsaw puzzles when you were a kid? I did. It was fun and often frustrating to put together that big picture that had been carefully sliced into 10,000 pieces.

Most people start by putting the edges together, which creates the framework. As you work from the outside in and move the pieces around, what seems complex at first becomes simpler as the big picture emerges. But it's practically impossible to do if you don't see the big picture first.

When you look at the front of the box and see the big picture, everything starts to make sense, and you can find the right pieces and lock them in their place. And who hasn't tried to force a piece in a spot where it doesn't fit?

So what does this mean for you today, right now? I submit to you, my friend, that this is the year, the moment, the minute, and the second when all the disjointed pieces of your puzzle are coming together.

There are many pieces to your life's puzzle. Pieces of a relationship that went south, a job that has sucked you dry and left you with nothing more to give, or perhaps a decision you wish you could shift into reverse.

There are other pieces that represent the good decisions you've made regarding your relationships, your career, and your life. But I sense that some of you look at those scattered pieces and wonder what in the world is going on. What's the point of the not-so-pretty pieces?

Everything you've experienced is a piece of your life's puzzle—and they are all necessary pieces. And you, my friend, are a necessary piece of a bigger puzzle, of a bigger picture. Wherever you find yourself right now, that place is better because you brought your piece to complete the big picture.

Here's the point: In everything that you are and ever hope to be in life, your talent, gifts, and abilities are the missing piece of the puzzle that, when connected to the right situation, cause things to come alive and make a difference. It's like adding a pinch of salt or sprinkle of black pepper to a dish—you are the exact ingredient that is needed to make the recipe taste just right.

There are things that will never be complete until you show up with your brilliant piece of the puzzle. Your piece of the puzzle is the linchpin, the master key, the fuel in the engine, the code, the secret sauce, the solution to the problem, and the right answer at the right time.

I invite you, O' Brilliant One, to be thankful and to celebrate all of the pieces of your puzzle!

BRILLIANT DECREE

I am the missing piece of the puzzle. There is no other piece like me, and the puzzle is not complete without me in it.

BRILLIANT NEXT STEP

Notice which pieces of your puzzle represent your core strengths. Celebrate them and embrace them! Determine which puzzle pieces you still need to address. Visit a professional counselor, hire a certified coach, or meet with a family member to bring closure to pieces that may be out of place, and then decide what has to happen so that you can move forward with the rest of your life.

Refrain from judging your puzzle pieces. Just accept them.

INSIGHT 4
OWN YOUR CAREER

(Career/Business)

I was recently invited to speak at AT&T, IBM, Master-Card, and Microsoft. While there, I decided I would lean in and learn what they are telling their employees, which ultimately has a direct impact on their customers. The common thread can be summed up in this statement: *The adult day care center is officially closed; it's time for you to own your career.* Business is changing at the speed of light, and to keep the pace, you need to become your own *career architect.*

Technology is clearly driving this line of thinking. McKinsey & Company forecasted that, by 2025, automated technology innovations will do the tasks that are now performed by 250 million knowledge workers worldwide, which will free the rest of the workforce to devote their time and energy to more creative pursuits.

Think about it in the context of a typical day. You need a prescription and call the pharmacy. You follow a series of prompts but never actually talk to a live person. The technology is so advanced that when your prescription is ready, you receive a text message. The only time you interact with another human being is when you walk into the store and an employee says, "Welcome to Walgreens."

Just over a year after declaring a radical change in management style called holacracy—an approach to leadership that involves no job titles, no formal bosses, and overlapping work circles—Zappos CEO Tony Hsieh issued a memo that addressed how that change was progressing. He said that managers had been important and had contributed to the success of the company up to that point, but going forward, there would be a new world order—one of self-management. Those who didn't agree with this new direction could submit their resignation, and if they were in good standing with the organization, they would receive a three-month severance package.

This is exactly why every willing and able-bodied person must own their career!

Don't feel nervous about your career when you read about such changes. In fact, these kinds of changes make it the greatest time to be alive! They can be the catalysts to challenging yourself to do what you can to better yourself, so you're more valuable to the business and are relevant today and in the future.

BRILLIANT DECREE

I am a solution to the problems
that exist in this business.
I am one of the most sought-after
workers in my place of business.
I love my business and the
customers we serve.
I am leading a business that is in
the top 1 percent of its industry.

BRILLIANT NEXT STEP

Here are three strategies you can implement to own your career:

1. **Embrace Microlearning**—Lynda.com is the new face of learning for busy professionals. That's why LinkedIn paid $1.5 billion to acquire it. The Lynda.com platform is like Netflix for business. You can access and learn just about any skill in three- to five-minute blocks. For $25 per month, you can up your game and stay on the cutting edge. When you complete a course on Lynda.com, you receive a skill badge that you can post on your LinkedIn profile. This is gamification at its best.

2. **Create a Strategic Life Plan**—You either have to fulfill the vision of the system, or hack the system to fulfill your own vision. In ten years, you'll be older. The question is, will you be better? To ensure that you are, put together a strategic life plan that is broken down into one-year, three-year, and six-year goals. Your plan should address all seven core areas of your life—spiritual,

financial, emotional, mental, social, career/business, and wellness. Be specific about how you intend to execute this plan.

3. **Reinvent Your Job**—In my global travels, I have noticed that many professionals in middle management are redefining their roles within their organization and are giving up the roles that they've played for years. They are creating new positions for themselves, based on what they are most passionate about and what aligns with the future direction of the company. Because they are employees in good standing with brilliant reputations, they are being given the opportunity to do something new. It's similar to a start-up company. There is tremendous risk, no guarantees, and huge upside potential.

INSIGHT 5
UNLEASH YOUR INNER SALMON

(Mental)

Jennifer Bertoglio is the oldest of eight children. She grew up in Streeter, Illinois, a blue-collar town where people rarely went to college and upward mobility was a distant thought. As a child, she waited in rice lines and wore hand-me-down clothes, but she attributes her drive to succeed against all odds to her challenging upbringing.

Her first job out of college was as a contract employee for Amoco, but she put her persuasion skills in action and talked herself into a full-time job. She advanced quickly, and when she decided she wanted to go to law school, her employer believed in her and gladly paid for it.

When she finished law school, Jennifer was offered a secure corporate position as a litigator. The more she explored this option, the less comfortable she felt. That traditional opportunity did not align with her soul, so she walked away from it.

She went on to become a director of business development and a recruiter for a legal staffing company in Chicago. As she poured herself into this opportunity, Jennifer noticed something. A lot of lawyers who had incredible credentials had become marginalized. They barely made any money and were sitting on park benches wondering what their next move would be. Many had been downsized by the fluctuations in Corporate America and had kissed their six-figure salaries and bonuses goodbye. And yet, they were so capable.

Jennifer unleashed her power of metaconnection, and after she watched and listened to the plight of these lawyers, an idea emerged. She had found an answer. Jennifer created a new service, LawyerLink, which combined three industries—e-discovery services, legal processes onshoring with temporary legal staffing. From its humble beginnings of an office in her spare bedroom, where she used a folding table for her desk and invested $30,000 of her personal savings, she grew the company to 125 people, $10 million in gross revenue, and offices that occupied two floors of the Sears Tower (now the Willis Tower) in Chicago—in only five years!

LawyerLink's secret sauce was that they taught project management skills and six sigma principles to attorneys. Because they soon produced a better work product and attracted regular work from traditional law firms, Jennifer was able to sell LawyerLink to Axiom, a legal services marketplace disruptor, for an undisclosed amount.

Here are three lessons I learned from Jennifer Bertoglio:

1. *Transcend Your Environment*

Jennifer grew up in poverty, but she didn't let it define her or determine who she would become. She pulled herself up by the bootstraps, paid her way through college, and pursued her dream of making herself better.

This is not so unusual for any successful person. What makes Jennifer different is her spirit of philanthropy, which is rooted in her philosophy of *living to give instead of living only to get more.* She is doing more than just living; she and her husband are thriving by sharing.

2. Swim Upstream Against Popular Opinion

Men and women who recognize opportunity early and often are wired differently. Their divergent way of thinking causes them to ask questions and create solutions that others think are impossible. They refuse to be marginalized by insecure thinking. Jennifer disrupted the wingtip, buttoned-up, boys-only-club legal circles when she identified a pain point and solved it. She ignored the rules of engagement and swam in another lane—and she didn't need anyone's permission to be there.

3. Stay Thirsty

Jennifer has an unquenchable thirst to learn, and she does it through adventure travel. She and her husband have visited seventeen countries, and each destination became a living classroom that shaped their thinking about how they could make a global impact through their business ventures. Jennifer is constantly exploring the next industry to disrupt and apply the lessons she's learned to maximize present opportunities. Are you unlearning, relearning, and learning what empowers you to be relevant in the new global economy? It starts with a thirst to discover the unknown, the uncommon, and what seems out of the ordinary.

BRILLIANT DECREE

I am a brilliant thinker and doer.

I don't follow the crowd,
the crowd follows me.

I am finding new ways to stay
relevant and to grow my mind.

BRILLIANT
NEXT STEP

What will you do to rise above your surroundings and soar to new heights? You have a daily choice to create the future or react to the one created for you.

How does Jennifer's story inspire you to think about your path and your intent to live a brilliant life?

CREATE POSITIVE OUTCOMES

(Wellness)

I recently had dinner with J. Lennox Scott, Chairman and CEO of John L. Scott Real Estate, a third-generation real estate firm based in Seattle, Washington. I asked him, "What has caused your company to succeed in this economy?" He said that everything shifted when he challenged his employees to walk in joy, walk in abundance, and live an inspired life.

"Our company is not just a real estate company; we are a learning company," Lennox said. He requires all his executives to read a book together, then discuss how they will apply the techniques they learned. This practice has inspired their agents to improve themselves and stop settling for the status quo. The real estate business is a tough one, and with a thirty percent turnover rate among agents, the ones who survive do so because they possess all three of these key components—the right mindset, the skill level needed to compete, and the initiative to take action on his or her own behalf.

That's why Lennox hired a Vice President of Agent Excellence, whose sole responsibility is to help their agents maximize their performance. This role combines organizational development, human resources, and learning and development. The VP's mission is to help their agents discover possibilities, rather than focus on why they are not doing something. He challenges them by asking, "Why are we doing this activity?" and "How can we create a positive outcome?"

When I asked him how he defined a positive outcome, Lennox lit up like a Christmas tree.

"To get to the positive outcome," he said, "you have to make a positive contribution to the potential prospect or past client. It's not about what you get from them; it's about what you can give to them."

This method allows an agent to "walk in joy" because he or she knows that they are making a positive impact on the customer's life and are doing more than just buying or selling a home. "Walking in abundance" happens when an agent knows that he is making a positive contribution to his customers' lives and is worthy of earning a living from the problems he solves and the solutions he finds.

This was one of the most enlightening conversations I've had with Lennox, who understands that the greatest asset of any business beyond brick, mortar, and intellectual capital is their people.

BRILLIANT DECREE

Today, I am walking in joy.

Today, I am living in a
place of abundance.

Today, I am living an inspired life and
am inspiring everyone around me.

BRILLIANT NEXT STEP

1. Find out whether your team members possess the right mindset, skill level, and initiative to take action. If they are lacking in any of these areas, then you have your work cut out for you. You can also steer toward www.simontbailey.com for more development.

2. Be sure to tell your employees what they are doing right instead of what they are doing wrong. I like to recall this anecdote: A coach was yelling at a football player, telling him all the things he was doing wrong on the field, when another player observed the coach berating his teammate and said, "Coach, aren't you going to tell him how to do it right?"

3. Walk in joy. That's right. Every day you need to bounce out of bed with pep in your step because you have that day to create a moment for your team members. Thank them, nudge them to go the extra mile, give them an assignment that stretches their capabilities, then get out of their way.

INSIGHT 7
EXPAND YOUR ENVIRONMENT

 Mental

Harvey Mackay, author of the *New York Times* #1 best seller *Swim With the Sharks Without Being Eaten Alive,* shares a powerful insight about the Japanese Koi fish, which has unlimited growth potential—as long as it's in the right environment.

When the Koi fish lives in a small fish bowl, it will only grow to two or three inches. When it's put in a larger tank or even small pond, it will grow to six to ten inches. If it's placed in an even bigger pond, it will grow to one-and-a-half feet. And if the fish is put into a large lake where it can really stretch out, it will grow to three feet.

The size of the fish is proportional to the size of its environment.

The size of your future is only limited by the size of your quantum field.

Your spirit grows in direct proportion to the size of the environment in which you choose to live. Be audacious. What other choice do you really have in a world that craves conformity?

BRILLIANT DECREE

Every chance I have, I choose
to expand my environment
through constant learning. I
surround myself with people who
challenge me to be better.

BRILLIANT
NEXT STEP

Become an online learning addict. In the new normal, there is no excuse why a person shouldn't know something or possess a particular skill. There is a plethora of e-learning classes, webinars, and digital platforms to discover. As philosopher Eric Hoffer asserts, in times of change, the learners will inherit the earth. Get a learning fix at least once a week.

What podcast, course, or service can you consume today that will expand your knowledge?

INSIGHT 8
THE KEY TO TRANSFORMATION
IS RIGHT BELOW YOUR NOSE

(Mental)

The Bible says, "Death and life are in the power of the tongue." That's also true for wealth and poverty, success and failure, joy and worry, brilliance and mediocrity, and so on and so on.

O' Brilliant One, here's the truth: You become the sum total of everything that comes out of your mouth. I invite you to proclaim all the good that your future holds. This is your time to transform your limited thinking to unlimited thinking. This is your time to embrace an abundant mindset. This is your season to plant your feet, dig in your heels, and transform your world from the inside out.

> Your mouth is the door to
> your future. Your words are
> the keys that unlock it.

One of the greatest phenomena in the world is the transformation of a caterpillar into a butterfly. According to the Vancouver Aquarium Marine Science Centre, the caterpillar spins its cocoon from silk that is produced by the glands in its mouth. Simply put, the caterpillar lives in what was spit out of its mouth. Just chew on that thought for a moment!

I have examined the lives of successful people through personal conversations and by reading their biographies and have discovered that they have something in common. I call it linguistic brilliance. These people understand that their words are seeds that they sow in the soil of their own heart. Each day they think and behave in ways that nurture the seeds that have been sown. Henry Ford said it best, "If you think you can, you can. And if you think you can't, you're right."

My mother used to tell me, "If you can't say anything nice, don't say anything at all." That advice applies to what you say about yourself, too, and about your future. Death and life are in the power of the tongue. Speak life!

If you want to transform your life, your job, or your business, I invite you to examine your speech. Make it positive, make it prosperous, make it grateful, make it truthful, make it encouraging, and make it the bedrock by which you live. Create your future by speaking it into existence.

BRILLIANT DECREE

I choose my words carefully. I speak well of other people. My words carry the very essence of my spirit and, as a result, my words bless the lives of others. God is pleased when I speak well of his creations.

BRILLIANT
NEXT STEP

o Write a letter to yourself dated one year from today and describe where you intend to be. Write it in past tense as if it is already done.

o Purge these words from your vocabulary: don't, not, stop, can't, won't, should've, would've, and could've.

o Be mindful about what you say, and always be quick to listen.

INSIGHT 9
CHANGE—A BRILLIANT OPPORTUNITY TO GROW!

(Financial)

Absolutely everything is in a continuous state of change.

Seeds sown into soil change to produce a plant, a tree, or a beautiful flower. Children undergo profound changes as they mature into adults. Even inanimate objects like rocks change as they are buffeted by wind and rain.

As in life, change is the natural state of business. Anyone who does not change with the times will eventually become obsolete and irrelevant, out of step with the strategic direction of their organization.

Could that be you?

I've seen people adopt one of three different personas when confronted with change: the Skeptic, the Fence-sitter, or the Supporter. Which one are you?

Skeptics have a mindset that says, "This too shall pass!" They think the change is nothing more than "the flavor of the month," and don't think it pertains to them. They appear to go along with the change, but in the back of their minds, they know it won't work. To prove their point, they speak out against new initiatives. During meetings, they are present in body but absent in mind. They are mentally somewhere else because they don't accept change. Skeptics have a limited future and may be invited to find their happiness and paycheck elsewhere.

This is not a wake-up call—it's a direct slap in the face. Change or be changed!

Fence-sitters either support change immediately or wait until later on when it's the politically correct and safe thing to do, or when their personal gain is at stake. If an enterprise-wide change has no direct impact on what they put in their own pocket, it means very little to them. This attitude will stunt their professional growth.

My advice to them is simple: Get off the fence. Embrace the change for who you will become rather than what you will get.

Supporters "get it." They don't need to understand how the change will affect them in order to appreciate why it's important. Their desires, demeanors, and dispositions support the positive aspects of change, and their approach to change is collaborative, considerate, and consistent. Supporters behave in a manner that sends the message that they agree in mind and spirit. They do not wallow in skepticism or fence-sitting.

Which one are you? Decide today that you will change or be changed by change.

BRILLIANT DECREE

I welcome change. I am ready for change. I will bless it and not curse it. As I do, I will develop the ability to stay nimble, relevant, and skillful, even during times of uncertainty.

BRILLIANT NEXT STEP

Search your heart. If you realize you can never be a Supporter, perhaps it's time to find your brilliance elsewhere. If, on the other hand, you choose to emotionally commit to change, and I do hope that's your choice, demonstrate that you're on board with your leaders and your organization through your behavior.

o Raise your hand and volunteer to help instead of waiting for others to do the work.

o Offer workable ideas and suggestions.

o Be proactive and go the extra mile.

o Stop talking about saving money and do it.

INSIGHT 10
HUG YOUR TREE AND BOUNCE BACK

(Mental)

My friend Robin Rampersad said something that totally rocked my world. His eyes were on fire as he shared this powerful nugget of truth. He said, "When a tree is going through its winter season, it can't produce its food via the process of photosynthesis. That changes everything for the tree because a tree traps sunlight in its leaves via the chlorophyll and transforms it, along with other viable ingredients, into its food."

In winter, the normal mode is not an option because there isn't enough sunlight to produce food, nor are there any leaves to trap the sunlight. As a result, instead of being flush with fruits and leaves, the tree appears outwardly dead.

The tree is forced to find food another way. It has to turn inward. And here is the brilliance of God. The tree pushes its roots deep into the soil, searching for minerals, salts, and water to sustain itself. The tree anchors itself more and more deeply so that it will be able to produce even more fruit and bounty the next season. The fruit will be a better quality because the nutrients have come from deep within the recesses of the earth.

A tree cannot grow bigger or go deeper until the winter season, which requires it to change everything it knows how to do.

Perhaps, like this tree, you've been forced out of your normal routine. Perhaps you, too, are experiencing a winter season.

When you find yourself in a dormant state, make the most of it. Push yourself to go deeper, to learn more, to prepare for the next opportunity, the next growth season. Become desperate, not in the sense of despairing, but in the sense of doing more, of going deeper, just like the tree in winter.

BRILLIANT DECREE

When I cannot control my environment or when progress slows to a near standstill, I do everything in my power to prepare for a better future.

BRILLIANT
NEXT STEP

Be desperate. Go deep. Learn a new skill. Seek a different path. Be a better friend. Give until it returns to you.

INSIGHT 11
FOCUS FOR SUCCESS

Career/Business

An archery teacher placed a wooden bird in a field and asked his students to aim at the eye of the bird.

He asked the first student, "What do you see when you take aim?" The student said, "I see the trees and their branches and leaves. I see the sky. And I see the bird and its eye."

The teacher turned to his second student and asked, "And what do you see?" The second student said, "I see only the eye of the bird." "Very good," said the teacher. "Take your shot."

The arrow flew straight and hit the bird directly in its eye.

Until you focus, my friend, you cannot hit the target!

Whatever you are moving toward, that goal is also moving toward you. What is your focus right now? Do you believe in it? Whatever you're aiming for, put your head, heart, and hands into it.

BRILLIANT DECREE

I am intentional with my time and energy. I am like a laser in my daily efforts rather than a floor lamp that diffuses its energy or a strobe light that doesn't focus on any particular thing.

BRILLIANT
NEXT STEP

Focus comes, in part, from leading a simplified life. Does that surprise you? Perhaps you thought that going above and beyond requires you to multitask. Current research confirms that when you multitask, you are actually less efficient, not more.

According to author Edward Willett, "When you do two things at once, brain power doesn't increase to meet demand; in fact, it decreases, which means you perform each task more poorly than if you focused on one alone."

Here are a couple of tips for focusing:

1. Determine your rhythm—those times when you're most alert and in the zone. Dr. Lothar Seiwert, a simplicity expert, says: "Identify your highly productive periods and root out inner time thieves by writing down your work schedule for the week. Work on your difficult assignments during those productive times."

2. De-mystify complex tasks and projects by breaking them down into bite-sized chunks. Then focus on one chunk at a time.

Doing so allows you to focus on the details that drive exceptional and unexpected results. Multitaskers don't devote their full attention to the work at hand, and they often don't take the time to fully understand the breadth and depth of a project, thereby getting only mediocre results.

INSIGHT 12
HACK YOUR LEADERSHIP STYLE

(Career/Business)

A Harvard Business Review study found that around one-third of a company's profitability is impacted by its leadership style. So how do you cultivate a leadership style that works?

If you employ only one style of leadership, your organization may not be able to adapt to today's dynamic business environment and sustain profitability. An effective leader has to "bait the hook to suit the fish." They assess each situation and are flexible so they can meet their goals.

Conventional Styles of Leadership

Traditional leadership styles have long been taught. Some of these include:

The Autocratic Leader

This leader makes business decisions without involving his or her subordinates. Their style allows them to make quick decisions, and typically leads to close supervision of employees, but it may lead to employee dissatisfaction.

The Transactional Leader

This leader works with their employees, and they agree to pursue their mutual preplanned goals. The manager has full autonomy to reward or punish his or her subordinates. This style clarifies the responsibilities of both parties and ensures fair practice of work, but it can inhibit creativity at the lower levels.

The Transformational Leader

A transformational leader inspires his/her employees via high levels of communication, and expects a high level of productivity. Employees are given clear responsibilities and are expected to deliver the best results. This style can help boost job morale and employee satisfaction.

Modern Approaches to Leadership

Here's the thing: Leadership is never static. In order for you and your employees to remain effective, your leadership style must evolve. If you don't hack your style, your particular approach, whatever it is, will stop working. Here are three actions that will help you become an effective leader:

1. *Evaluate your workers*

A good leader adopts a style that meets the conditions of the workplace and the characteristics of subordinates. You must learn what works best for *them*. Bait the hook to catch the fish.

2. Understand your business model and needs

To be an effective leader, your business model and departmental needs must be considered. For instance, a fast-food manager has to make quick decisions, so he/she may adopt a slightly less democratic leadership style than a bank manager, where strong communications and interpersonal skills are important.

3. Anticipate future trends

In the long term, you may have to drop the autocratic style and develop a participative style of leadership. Studies conducted across many different countries show that workers everywhere are seeking fewer restrictions and more recognition. They want to have more control over their work.

The one-size-fits-all leadership approach is a thing of the past. Flexibility and adaptability are critical for modern leadership. That's how you hack your leadership style!

BRILLIANT DECREE

I am an emotionally intelligent leader.

I am the leader whom everyone wants to work for, collaborate with, and engage in innovative solutions.

I seek to serve everyone, and I give credit to the team for the results they produce.

BRILLIANT
NEXT STEP

Find a team member today and tell them what they did right.

Have a career investment discussion with your team members by finding out what makes them tick and what they want to accomplish in their life.

Ask your team members what you can do to become a better leader for them.

Ask your peer leaders and manager what you can do to help them succeed.

INSIGHT 13
PROACTIVE FEEDBACK IS THE GREATEST GIFT

Career/Business

It's been said that feedback is a gift.

While that's certainly true, I think it's only half the story. I believe that *proactive feedback is an even better gift*.

Let me share a short story to make my point.

I recently had a large client engagement, and I asked a colleague to facilitate some of the sessions. She graciously agreed and adjusted her own business schedule to accommodate my client's needs. But as things progressed, I began to sense that the client was going to increase the scope of the project, which would dramatically alter my colleague's involvement.

Instead of keeping her abreast of the potential changes, I didn't say anything about it. There were a number of reasons why I didn't, and I now realize that none of them were particularly good ones. When the client finally made the decision I was anticipating, I called my colleague and dropped the bomb. She was polite and professional, said, "Okay," and we hung up.

She called me back a few minutes later and said, "I need to give you some feedback." She pointed out that I had withheld information that was crucial to her business. Needless to say, she was right, and I was clearly wrong. With no place to hide, after a long pause I cried "uncle" and took full responsibility for not sharing the information with her earlier.

Feedback is a gift. Proactive feedback is an even greater gift.

My colleague's feedback was a gift. The next time I bring someone else in on a project, you can be sure I'll communicate in a timely manner and clarify the expectations. It would have been an even greater gift if I'd given her proactive feedback about the possible changes—if I'd actually done that. Despite the fact that my actions had a negative impact on her business, she graciously allowed me to stretch and grow yet again, and I thank her.

BRILLIANT DECREE

Today I welcome open and honest feedback. I will carefully evaluate this feedback and make the necessary adjustments. Receiving feedback will become an ongoing habit, and I will seek it out on a quarterly basis.

BRILLIANT
NEXT STEP

Seek proactive feedback from your leaders, coworkers, significant others, family members, and friends. Feedback is powerful! It's a tool that measures where we are, where we need to go, and what we might be doing that sabotages our efforts to close the gap.

Whenever you receive feedback, write it down in your journal so you can track how you develop over time.

Consider some of the following:

Give feedback to someone else.

A direct report, a coworker, a spouse, a child, a friend. Give them feedback because you care and because you want to help them realize their full potential and release their brilliance.

Find it for yourself.

If no one gives you feedback on a regular basis, be proactive. Seek it out. Find people who care about you and ask them these questions:

1. In what areas do I need to improve?
2. Do you see areas of strength that I can leverage?
3. What can I do to exceed your expectations?

INSIGHT 14
A NEW ERA TO BE DYNAMIC

Career/Business

I remember my very first performance evaluation early in my corporate career. I sat across from my boss, looked her in the eyes, and waited for the accolades I thought I deserved. I had done everything that had been asked of me and had tried really hard to do a good job. Unlike my colleagues who dreaded this moment, I was more than ready to hear how great I was.

Imagine my disappointment when I received average, middle-of-the-road scores. I was devastated. Before I could ask her why I wasn't at the top of the scale, she congratulated me for doing a good job and for being a great contributor.

Then it came. She said, "Before your next evaluation, I want to encourage you to take it to the next level, to initiate more, and show us you can do more than just what's expected." In other words, she was telling me that there was nothing spectacular about doing a good job. That was what was expected. It's what I was paid to do. It was a strong message, and I've never forgotten it.

I invite you to answer this very important question: What will you personally do to add value to your company and to take your performance to the next level? I submit to you that *it's time to be dynamic!*

Here's the deal: When life gets bumpy, it's time to rise to a new altitude. That new altitude is summed up in two words:

Be dynamic.

You know it, and I know it. You were born to be the very best at whatever you set your mind to. If you are a mother, then be a dynamic mother. If you are a bank teller, then be a dynamic teller. If you are a salesperson, then be a dynamic salesperson. Mediocrity is the antithesis of dynamic living.

You are capable of leaving a significant imprint rather than a fleeting impression. Those who determine to be dynamic in whatever they do, leave an imprint. You see it in every field of study, every industry, every vocation. Look through the annals of history, and you see men and women who rose to the occasion, and we still talk about them today. Why? Because they decided that mediocrity was for those who choose to live at a low altitude.

Whatever you do and wherever you find yourself at this season of your journey, open the vault of your potential and determine to be dynamic every day, in every way.

BRILLIANT DECREE

I was born to be dynamic. I will act dynamic, talk dynamic, look dynamic, and think dynamic. I will raise the bar in all areas of my life.

BRILLIANT
NEXT STEP

As a leader, shadow one of your team members each month or once per quarter. Learn through their lens what is happening in real time.

As a team member, ask another team member what you can take off their plate so that they can achieve their goal.

Decide how you will go the extra mile for a customer.

CREATE YOUR OWN PERSONAL BOARD OF DIRECTORS

(Family)

Your personal Board of Directors doesn't refer to a few high-ranking, intellectual individuals who advise your company on crucial matters. *It refers to that group of people who inspire you, motivate you, and challenge you to think beyond yourself.*

These are the people whose advice you seek about important personal and professional matters, and who always keep your head straight. But how do you create your personal Board of Directors?

Choose Those Who Inspire

The purpose of a personal Board of Directors is to gain insight and wisdom from people you respect. As we progress in our lives, both personally and professionally, we meet a number of people who become our teachers. They become an important source of enlightenment. Expand your inner circle to include those who challenge your thinking and stimulate you to greater heights of brilliance.

Choose Diversity

How much do you think you can learn from someone who is exactly like you? Maybe a little, but probably not a lot. Include people who have inspired you, despite their starkly different personalities, their different ways of thinking, and their unique paradigms. The more people you include who have different approaches, the more you will learn.

In a similar vein, cross over different age brackets. Include some who are younger than you, some who are older, and others who are the same age. Create a mix of professional backgrounds and various fields to add diverse perspectives.

Pick at Least One Person Who Knows You Well

Someone who knows your temperament, your style of thinking, and your ambitions is in a good position to advise you and to give honest feedback. Even if they don't add much in terms of creativity or diversity, it's always good to have a trusted individual on your Board.

Be On the Lookout

Always be on the lookout for people who might be a good addition to your circle. If you meet someone new, and they strike you as being an enlightening source, don't hesitate to include him or her. Remember, two heads are better than one, and in this case, this adage goes a long way.

O Brilliant One, it's time for you to think about creating your personal Board of Directors.

BRILLIANT DECREE

I am surrounded by brilliant men and women who stretch me and invite me to grow.

I learn from every one of my relationships.

I am listening more and talking less.

BRILLIANT
NEXT STEP

Find three to five people who challenge your
thinking. Only one of them should be in a similar job, role, or business. Find people from
other industries so they can challenge you to
see things through their lens of the world.

INSIGHT 16
RESPECT HAS NO BOUNDARIES

(Social)

When you make a daily decision to be open, to genuinely listen, and to suspend judgment of others, life gets amazing. Not too long ago, our family was visiting the San Diego Zoo, and while we were in the Rain Forest Aviary, a father heard us call our daughter, whose name is Madison. As it turned out, he also had a daughter named Madison.

This serendipitous connection led to a truly memorable day. As we watched, the girls built an instant and easy friendship. It was already clear that they were going to be inseparable, so we decided to get to know each other's family.

We learned that Boomer and his wife, Bonnie, were from a small town of fewer than 2,000 people outside of Billings, Montana. He was in the mining business, and she was a nurse. For the next couple of hours, we toured the zoo together. We barely looked at the animals because we were so busy asking questions and learning about each other's lives.

It was amazing! We learned that we thought along the same lines when it came to the taboo topics of religion and politics. It didn't matter that we were from the city, while they were from the country. We suspended whatever hang-ups we might have had because our daughters were playing and talking together as if they had known each other for years.

As we said our goodbyes, the girls exchanged phone numbers and promised to stay in contact. We traded e-mail addresses with the parents and told them we'd keep in touch. Then we mentioned that we wanted to take our son on a fly-fishing trip soon. Without batting an eye, Boomer said, "If you ever fly into Montana, let us know. We'll pick you up from the airport, and you can stay at our house."

What a priceless experience! How uplifting it was to be the recipient of such generosity! Whether we ever see Boomer, Bonnie, and Madison again, one thing is for sure: I am convinced now more than ever that respect, courtesy, and kindness have no boundaries.

BRILLIANT DECREE

Every day in every way, I will be
kind to those who can do nothing
for me. I will stand up for those who
cannot stand up for themselves.
One day someone will stand up
for me when I least expect it and
need it the most. I am brilliant.

BRILLIANT
NEXT STEP

What will you do to extend yourself to others?
Are there some people you need to connect
with to have a cup of coffee or lunch? What
new connections will you make to enrich your
life and theirs?

INSIGHT 17
BREAK YOUR CRUTCHES

(Mental)

Have you ever said to yourself:

I talk funny. It can't be done.

I have NO support. No one believes in me.

I am stuck. I am too old. No one will ever marry me.

I am too set in my ways. It has never been done before.

Will anyone purchase my product or service?

I will forgive but never forget.

Why does this always happen to me? I guess this is the way it's supposed to be.

I have three years until I retire.

I am going to play it safe and not rock the boat.

These phrases are all crutches. They're excuses for you to stay small, to curl up in your comfort zone and keep you from going after your heart's desire.

I know that I'm writing to someone who needs to hear these words. Is it you?

I was flying through the Dallas/Fort Worth Airport and observed a woman on crutches. Her left foot was in a cast, and all of her support came from her right leg. She couldn't carry anything except a purse that was slung over her shoulder. She was totally focused on what was immediately in front of her as she navigated her way through the terminal.

The look on her face was a heartbreaking mixture of distress, anxiety, and helplessness. When she finally found a seat, she hopped on one leg as she swung herself around and gently sat down. She put her crutches in the chair next to her and let out a long sigh.

Then it hit me. What happens when people become trapped, dependent, and stuck on mental and emotional crutches? There comes a point when you have to let go of your self-imposed limitations and throw away the crutches and all the excuses that hold you back and keep you down. Enough is enough! Reach toward all that is possible and muster the courage and confidence to go for it!

BRILLIANT DECREE

Today I release the crutches of self-doubt, low self-esteem, wavering confidence, and purposelessness. I will no longer hobble around using the same old tired excuses about why I can't do anything to improve my life.

BRILLIANT
NEXT STEP

Think about your career and business. What crutches no longer serve you? Do you play it safe and refuse to speak up during meetings? Are you waiting for other people to invite you to the table, afraid you don't belong? It's high time, my friend, to stand on your own two feet. This is your moment.

REJECTION CAN BE THE GREATEST GIFT IN THE WORLD

(Emotional)

I recently received a rejection e-mail from a business agent that said, "I'm so sorry. They did not select you this year. Their terrible loss!!! I will suggest you again in another proposal next year."

I wrote back, "This is exciting news. I am so happy you told me that I wasn't selected. Now I'm going to take my game to the next level." What my agent didn't know was that this was the ninth year in a row I'd been rejected by this particular group. Two other agents had already pitched me to this organization.

Even though I answered that e-mail in a matter of seconds and was positive about it, as the reality sank in, my disappointment was unsettling. This had taken the wind out of my sails, so to calm myself, I re-read the book *The Game of Life and How to Play It,* written in 1925 by Florence Shinn.

In the book, Shinn makes this powerful statement: *"The thing man seeks is seeking him—the telephone was seeking the bell."* All of sudden, it clicked: This was my invitation to shift from average thinking to brilliant living. I had been seeking something that wasn't seeking me. I needed to let it go and open up to what wanted to emerge and, more importantly, what belonged to me.

Faced with this disheartening situation, I did this: I chose to bless the decision makers with positive words, and I wished a brilliant future to all those who had been selected. I encourage you to do the same.

BRILLIANT DECREE

Today, I choose to bless everyone who has ever rejected me and to wish them a brilliant future. I will not dwell on negative emotions that arise from rejection. Instead, I will focus on the positives.

BRILLIANT
NEXT STEP

Any time you are faced with a disappointing experience, ask yourself what you can learn and how you will grow.

PERSONAL ACCOUNTABILITY IS YOUR POINT OF DIFFERENTIATION

(Career/Business)

We live in a time when people who work for large legacy brand companies (like IBM, Disney, JCPenney, Wal-Mart, and AT&T, to name a few) must find a way to stand above the crowd. You must find a way to escape the sea of sameness and realize that tenure alone doesn't guarantee your future employment. In the spirit of Jerry Maguire, "Show me the money!" If you want to survive for another quarter, you'd better deliver results.

In the early part of my sales career, I often thought that the name of the company I worked for would sell itself and, as a clipboard hugger, my job was to simply write the order, probe lightly by talking about family, weather, and sports, then get out of there as quickly as possible.

One day my boss told me that I was losing market share and that the big guys from corporate were scrutinizing every salesperson's individual production. Suddenly, I realized that producing was not going to be a walk in the park, and I needed to be personally accountable to turn things around.

One key character trait that each of us must develop is *personal accountability*. Personal accountability means that you take responsibility for your actions, above and beyond what is expected or required.

It's time to step up to the plate of personal accountability. Be responsible for yourself, for your family, for your company, and for your community. It's *your* job to make them better, no one else's. As I've said before, meeting expectations simply isn't enough anymore.

Here's a test: If you were putting a team together, would you hire yourself?

People who achieve great things go the extra mile because they want to, because they are accountable to themselves. Personal accountability isn't about a paycheck, a bonus, or the end game. It's about stretching yourself and pushing yourself to learn and grow. Practicing personal accountability is fulfilling and, yes, it's satisfying.

You are responsible for producing work that matters. Big Brother shouldn't have to look over your shoulder to see if you consistently focus on the right activities, use the company's time wisely, and spend the company's resources prudently. When you were hired, in effect, you agreed to an unwritten rule that you would take personal responsibility for your actions and represent the organization in a positive light at all times.

BRILLIANT DECREE

Today I choose to be accountable for everything I do, say, and think. As a result, I will be more productive with my time and more efficient with my energy.

BRILLIANT NEXT STEP

What is the greatest need where you work or in your life?

What is one simple step that you can take to be a solution to the problem?

Surprise and delight your customers. Do something positive they wouldn't expect, such as sending them a handwritten note or a video e-mail, or simply call them to thank them for their business.

INSIGHT 20
FLIP THE SCRIPT

(Mental)

A fifty-two-year-old man called in during a radio show and told the host, "I am out of a job, and you know that no man at fifty-two years of age can get a job. Furthermore, I don't have any brains. I haven't had any good experiences in life. I don't have any education, and no one likes me. What are you going to tell me to do about it?"

Dr. Norman Vincent Peale, the host of the show, said, "How do you know you don't have any brains?"

The man replied, "When I was young, I was told I didn't have any brains. All of the brains in the family went to my brother!"

Dr. Peale asked, "Who said that to you?"

The man replied, "My brother."

Peale then asked, "Who doesn't like you?"

The man said, "No one."

Peale said, "Do you like yourself?"

The man said, "I never thought I was supposed to like myself since I didn't have any brains."

Sounds pretty hopeless, no?

But amazingly, six weeks later, the same man sent a note to Dr. Peale and said he had landed a job. It wasn't much of a job, but he believed that he would take what he had been given and turn it into something significant. He said he was going to work until his job became great.

That fifty-two-year-old man flipped the script. He had hauled himself out of his hole of self-pity and began to challenge the things that had limited his life.

You flip the script when you ferret out and delete the viruses from your mind drive and heart drive that have crippled your operating system. When you flip the script, you reset your internal thermostat to be brilliant and watch your life rise to the new temperature.

Like that fifty-two-year-old man, something clicks inside of you, and you say, "Wait a minute. I have a choice to stand up and live or lie down and die."

Is it time for you to flip the script? To walk, talk, or think another way? I say, take control of your inner steering wheel!

BRILLIANT DECREE

I choose to flip the script, to take
control of the steering wheel
of my life and drive into the
future, instead of being driven by
everything and everyone else.

BRILLIANT
NEXT STEP

Grow the economy of your mind. The greatest asset you possess is your thinking. Dream big. Envision even bigger. Right now, yes, right now!

Read uplifting books and articles on Flipboard, a cool iPad app. Surround yourself with diverse thinkers. Take a look at your inner circle. Does everyone look like you, think like you, and talk like you? If so, then you may be limited to what they know. Learn another language. As the world shifts before our eyes, we need to be equipped with anything and everything that keeps us relevant.

INSIGHT 21
KINDNESS WILL IMPACT YOUR BOTTOM LINE

Spiritual

Og Mandino, author of *The Greatest Salesman in the World*, once said, "Beginning today, treat everyone you meet as if they were going to be dead by midnight. Extend to them all the care, kindness and understanding you can muster, and do it with no thought of any reward. Your life will never be the same again."

That nugget of wisdom is priceless. The secret to building a brilliant business is to build it on *kindness*.

When you build your business on kindness, it permeates your entire organization. It impacts the people you hire and the customers you serve. You not only make sales, but you make friends. That's brilliant!

When kindness is the foundation of your business, not only do your employees and customers appreciate it, but they also become your unofficial marketing department. They tell others about your brilliance, your kindness, and the authenticity of your business.

Here are five tips for building a foundation of kindness that will impact your bottom line:

1. **Examine Your Purpose**. Be in business to make meaning in addition to making money. To paraphrase the book *Firms of Endearment,* today's most successful companies bring

love, joy, authenticity, empathy, and soulfulness into their businesses. They deliver emotional, experi-
ential, and social value, not just profit. What is your
company's purpose and how is it expressed?

2. **Spread the Love**. The truth is that everyone wants
to feel loved, and they know it when they don't. Find
a way to exceed your customer's hopes and dreams.
Listen to them, ask questions, surprise and delight
them with the smallest things. Call five clients
whom you haven't spoken to for a while, but don't
ask them for anything. Just let them know that you
were thinking of them and wanted to say hello.

3. **Pursue Significance, and Success Will Follow**.
All over the planet, people are waking up to the
fact that success is empty, but significance is fulfilling. Success is fleeting, and significance is last-
ing. After the applause ends and dust collects on
the award, success is empty. However, significance
is a constant companion that reminds you to serve
all, love everyone, and never take anyone for grant-
ed. Success may come as the result of your position,
an acquisition, or fulfilling an unmet need, but significance is at work behind the scenes when no one
is looking, and it knows that it's better to give than
to receive.

4. **Forgive and Move On**. Stop crying over spilled
milk. It happened. Let it go and move on. You are
wasting precious energy trying to fix or change
someone or something. It is what it is. The future

will move toward you when you let go of the things that have been holding onto you. Let go.

5. **Ask, "What Else Can I Do for You?"** This simple question shows that you are going the extra mile. What does this look like in your business? Seek opportunities to anticipate unspoken needs in the business relationship. This could make a brilliant difference and produce unexpected results.

BRILLIANT DECREE

> I am kind.
> I am caring and careful about how I treat everyone.
> I gladly help those who can do nothing for me.

BRILLIANT NEXT STEP

Determine where you may have fallen short of being kind in your relationships. Now go back and repair them.

INSIGHT 22
APPETITE FOR THE SPECTACULAR

Wellness

When you become intentional about your life, nothing can stop you from creating your future. Is that your mantra for this year?

A friend of mine and I were talking at Starbucks, where all serious and important meetings take place. I asked her how she was doing and she said, "Simon, I have an appetite for the spectacular!" When she said that, I thought *Whoa...that is profound!* I couldn't get to my laptop fast enough to pound out those timeless words.

And that got me thinking. What does an appetite for the spectacular look like, sound like, taste like, talk like, feel like, and act like?

Here are some thoughts to meditate on...

Good is no longer good enough. If it's not spectacular, I am not interested. Life is to be enjoyed to the fullest, not just merely tolerated.

A job is what you are paid to do, but you were made to release your brilliance. If you are not releasing your brilliance, igniting your creative energy, or being a game changer where you work, then quit. Move on. Do something else. Fire yourself before you get fired.

If you're thinking, "I have bills to pay. I can't just quit," then transfer to a new department, sell your business, or cultivate a new attitude. If you are already doing a spectacular job, congratulations! If not, then you're in a job that someone else needs.

Surround yourself with 360-degree thinkers so you can learn to think and see like them. When you surround yourself with small thinkers, you will only think and see small! Bill Taylor, one of the founders of *Fast Company,* said it best, "Most companies in most industries have a kind of tunnel vision. They chase the opportunities that everyone else is chasing; they miss the opportunities that everyone else is missing. It's the companies that see a different game that win big."

Sell out to your dream, to your destiny, and to your desire to be brilliant. No more wandering around, waiting to be discovered. Discover yourself! Be your own American Idol, hold your arms up, and dance with the star that is you. Your future demands it.

BRILLIANT DECREE

I am first class. I choose to be
spectacular and to seek what
is spectacular in all things.
I choose to experience the
best that life has to offer.

BRILLIANT
NEXT STEP

Make a reservation at the best restaurant in town. Get dressed up and go out and experience it. Take a picture. Post it, share it, and look at it often. That's how special you are, O' Brilliant One.

INSIGHT 23
OVER-DELIVER

(Career/Business)

Part of the joy and challenge of being a parent is to teach our children to go above and beyond in everything they do and to help them find a way to go far beyond what's expected in every situation.

I recently listened to the woes of a business associate. She was exasperated with her twelve-year-old daughter's seeming unwillingness to do anything more than exactly what was asked of her. My friend had been a very different kind of child. She had been a textbook overachiever and people pleaser from birth. She couldn't understand why, when she asked her daughter to pick up her school stuff in the living room, that she ONLY picked up her backpack and homework, not the cup of juice or snack that sat beside her backpack. Her daughter's answer: "You just said 'school stuff'!"

Life gets more complex as we get older, but it is still possible to exceed expectations, despite the gravitational pull to be average. No matter what your responsibilities, accelerate your actions above and beyond what is expected or required. It really is possible.

In other words, show some "drive and some oomph." It simply isn't enough to meet expectations anymore. If you only do what is required, are you doing your best?

Not likely. Doing the bare minimum translates to being average, mediocre—just like everyone else.

People who achieve great things push themselves to go the extra mile, not because they have to or because someone makes them, but because they want to. They over-deliver. This becomes their personal signature. Think about what you can do to give something extra without seeking anything in return.

BRILLIANT DECREE

I know the importance of going
the extra mile, and I strive
to create uncommon, unique,
and exquisite experiences for
those I serve and for myself.

BRILLIANT
NEXT STEP

Identify one thing you can do to exceed expectations on a project or to move forward on an idea that you've been thinking about for a while.

INSIGHT 24
AMBIGUITY IS YOUR
GREATEST OPPORTUNITY

(Spiritual)

Have you ever had days when you look around and wonder what is going on? Have you ever asked yourself what is really important? How do you know if what you do really matters?

In the midst of this ambiguity, you must pay attention to what is happening around you. Alexander Graham Bell was a gifted pianist, and he also paid attention. He noticed that when he struck a chord on a piano in one room, it would be echoed by the piano in another room. He observed that entire chords could be transmitted through the air, which would vibrate the piano strings in another room at exactly the same pitch. This simple observation led him to invent the telephone.

Ambiguity can be a tool that pushes you to ask difficult questions.

The following questions can help push you through ambiguity to obtain brilliant clarity:

1. Where have you been? (Assess your experiences, your education, and your life journey.)

2. Why are you here? (Determine what choices, decisions, and opportunities brought you to this point.)

3. What can you do? (What skills will you cultivate to grow?)

4. Where are you going? (What snapshots flicker on the movie screen of your mind?)

Your new future is waiting to emerge. It can only break through when you admit that you don't know what you don't know, and when you remain open to learn and to grow.

BRILLIANT DECREE

Right now, I am the solution that someone else desperately needs. Right now, I am the answer to a problem. When I feel unsure of myself, I will stop and reflect to get myself back on track.

BRILLIANT
NEXT STEP

Share your answers to those four questions
(p. 155-156) with your accountability partner.

INSIGHT 25
CELEBRATE THE CRUMBS

(Mental)

When I left Disney more than a decade ago, I had huge dreams of becoming a *New York Times* best-selling author, of speaking to packed stadiums of eager listeners (who would soak in all the wisdom and motivation I was itching to share), and of creating an institute of motivation that would spread positivity and knowledge on an ongoing basis. My destiny was calling, and Easy Street awaited, right? Not so much.

It didn't take long for reality to set in. It's hard to be an entrepreneur. It was only after many long years of hard work and tremendous financial sacrifice that the picture I held in my head came close to the reality of my new life. That's the good news; the reality finally did match my dreams, and at times it has exponentially exceeded even my most spectacular hopes!

The same will be true for you, but here's the question: What do you do in the meantime, when your internal dream of success is the stark opposite of the current reality?

Here's what I did, and what I suggest for you. Focus on the details that will lead you where you want to go; extend a helping hand to whomever needs one; fuel your passions; become an expert in your field; seek a mentor. Gather the crumbs of your various experiences—your successes, your failures, your disappointments, your hopes, and your joys—and piece them together. Learn from them, and let them guide you. For it is these very crumbs that add flavor, substance, and texture to your dreams.

BRILLIANT DECREE

I am creating the future. I am gathering the crumbs of my experiences, and I am rolling them into a better tomorrow for my family, the world, and myself.

BRILLIANT
NEXT STEP

Develop an appetite for the spectacular instead of settling for the crumbs of the ordinary. Don't let negative people (the whiners and complainers) or your own negative thoughts influence you. Find inspiration from pictures in magazines and moments from daily life, and pin them on your Pinterest board.

INSIGHT 26
DISRUPTION IS YOUR NEW BFF

(Financial)

If you intend to live a brilliant life, then *disruption* is in your future. In fact, look at your calendar; it's your next appointment.

Disruption is one of the most important words to embrace in the 21st century. The disruption of our economy forced many of us to gain new perspectives in many areas, especially for our financial futures. There will come a time when you will have to break with the old to embrace the new, to let go of what is comfortable and convenient, in order to grow and expand.

Disruption leads to new discoveries, but only if you are open, present, and willing to pause and analyze what's really going on and to reflect on what you can learn from it. Disruptions provide an opportunity to refocus on what matters most, to de-clutter your heart, mind, and soul, and to uncover your hidden seeds of brilliance.

If you are doing things the way that you have always done them, then invite disruption in. You do not have the luxury of maintaining a wait-and-see attitude. That slow-moving strategy leads to becoming obsolete.

BRILLIANT DECREE

Change is my friend and not my foe. Change is a brilliant opportunity to grow. Change doesn't happen to me, it moves through me, and I become a better person as a result of it.

BRILLIANT
NEXT STEP

Answer the following questions:

1. When the next disruption takes place, which side of the fence will I be on?
2. Will I be the one who initiates the disturbance or the one who sits on the other side and watches it happen?
3. What do I have to break or split apart from in order to fly and soar?
4. What bold moves do I need to make in order to live my life by design rather than by default? How can I initiate a disruption?

INSIGHT 27
PUSH THROUGH THE WALL OF UNCERTAINTY

(Emotional)

"It is a gloomy moment in the history of our country. Not in the lifetime of most men has there been so much grave and deep apprehension; never has the future seemed as incalculable as at this time. The domestic economic situation is in chaos. Our dollar is weak throughout the world. Prices are so high as to be utterly impossible. The political cauldron seethes and bubbles with uncertainty. It is a solemn moment of our troubles. No man can see the end."
—*Harper's Weekly*, October 1857

Sound familiar? Could this have been written about the times *we* are living in? Maybe yes, maybe no. The truth is that each of us has a choice. We can either accept the gloom and doom, or we can reject it and keep pushing ahead.

O' Brilliant One, even in times of uncertainty, there are opportunities to be found, measures to take, and profits to earn.

If you intend to push through, you must first examine all the negative thoughts that are holding you back from your brilliant future. Assess all your relationships—are they assets or liabilities? Position yourself to punch through, push through, and kick through any barriers that confine you.

BRILLIANT DECREE

I am unstoppable. I am confident in my abilities, and uncertain times will not leave me hopeless and powerless. I am a winner. The only thing that can prevent me from winning is my own attitude.

BRILLIANT
NEXT STEP

After you determine which of your relationships are assets and which are liabilities,
make it your purpose to strengthen the former and let go of the latter. Ask yourself how
you can become the best person you can be.
Write your answers in a journal, and revisit it
every week.

INSIGHT 28
CHANGE THE CHANNEL

(Mental)

When I hear the echoes of global transformation in the current climate of turmoil and uncertainty, I can't help but think about my first visit to Uppsala, Sweden, a few years ago. After a two-hour plane ride from Moscow, I stood in line with seemingly hundreds of people from different parts of the world who were waiting to clear customs. I noticed that there were no worried looks on their faces, certainly not about the economy, either local or global.

Someway, somehow, the people in Sweden, whether they were residents or tourists, didn't get the memo and didn't buy into the idea that, even though North America was experiencing the fallout from the economy, that they should be shaking in their boots as well.

Here's the takeaway: It's time to change the channel. Simply put, when everyone else is screaming doom and gloom, don't buy into the hype. Choose to be positive and to be in control of what you hear and believe. Don't let negative news paralyze you.

BRILLIANT DECREE

> I will filter the images that appear on the television of my life. I will control the remote of my own thinking and change the channel if I need to.

BRILLIANT
NEXT STEP

Look at all of your life and figure out how you can look at it with a fresh perspective, as if you are seeing it for the first time.

Be intentional about how you hear and receive information. Listen carefully and determine what you will accept and what you will reject.

INSIGHT 29
WHERE'S YOUR SPARK?

(Family)

The mother of my two brilliant children is a candle lover, and she loves to light candles all around the house. The process of lighting candles and creating this ambience immediately puts her in a meditative, peaceful, Zen-like state, and everyone around her can feel it. We've watched the rare occasions when she can't get her special windproof lighter to spark properly. After a few futile strikes with no spark, the moment or "flow" of ambience seems to be lost.

Likewise, the presence or absence of a spark in your life can make or break the creation of something special. When you find your spark, it sets a series of events, circumstances, situations, and chance encounters in motion that I call "living in the flow."

A spark is a quality or talent that unleashes your energy and joy. When you invest your time and ability in something that is meaningful and is congruent with your internal wiring, it creates a spark. You become the match that starts a fire, which spreads from person to person, situation to situation, opportunity to opportunity.

When I finally discovered a simple truth about myself, that I exist at this specific period in time to do one specific thing—to inspire, instill and infuse hope in other human beings—I stopped trying to be like everyone else. I had lost myself at times in the past because I thought I had to say everything just right to make others value me. But that doesn't happen anymore.

When you find your inner spark, it allows your mojo, your essence, and your swag to fill a room. Why? Simply put, you are no longer in the room; the room is in you. You become present to the moment. You realize that you exist to *give* instead of *get*. Your spark becomes the push, the nudge, the shove that others need to find their own inner spark.

Bruce Barton, one of the founders of BBDO, one of the nation's largest advertising agencies, said it best: "If you have anything really valuable to contribute to the world, it will come through the expression of your personality, that single spark of divinity that sets you off and makes you different from every other living creature."

Where there is no spark, there is no joy. Where there is no joy, there is no hope; and where there is no hope, there is no passion. Without passion, a job is just a job. A marriage is just two roommates sleeping in the same bed and sharing bills while living under the same roof. A business is simply something to do instead of something that makes a difference in the world.

When you find your spark, you find your joy, and when you find your joy, you find freedom. And when you find freedom, you find your chutzpah.

Be the spark. Create the spark. Get moving and, for goodness' sake, don't stay stuck on a bridge to nowhere! Somewhere in the world, someone or something needs you to wake up and shift.

BRILLIANT DECREE

Today I choose to be a spark. I will create a spark, and my words will be the match that lights the fire in others around me. I will look for ways to merge my passions with the needs of society and others.

BRILLIANT
NEXT STEP

Today, walk into a place and smile. Light the room up with your presence. Tell someone you trust that if they catch you being negative, you will give them $20 on the spot to a charity of their choice.

OCCUPY THE MOMENT

(Wellness)

Are you waiting for your big break? If so, you're going to be waiting a long time.

The elusive "big break" isn't the result of good luck. It's the moment when preparation, opportunity, and occupancy meet. It's the moment when you stand on your own two feet and make something happen. No one is going to hold your hand, babysit you, or listen to lame excuses about why you won't step into your brilliance. It's up to you to do that.

This is the moment when you kick out the mental tenant of wait-and-see and invite in the new tenant, "Go and Get It." It's the moment when you send an instant message to your central nervous system that says, "I AM GOING TO MAKE THIS MOMENT COUNT!"

Dr. Daniel Kahneman, Professor Emeritus at Princeton University and Nobel Laureate, discovered that there are 19,200 moments in a day. When I first came across this brilliant factoid, a voice inside me said, *"A moment creates momentum, and momentum creates monumental results."*

If you don't make your own moments, then someone else will make them for you. If you don't have a vision, you will ultimately live out the vision of someone else.

You are the most important occupant of your future, and you cannot afford to let anyone or anything occupy your life unless they are making a direct contribution to your growth and development. You must make sure that your health and wellness is protected in every area: physically, mentally, emotionally, and spiritually. When you are prepared for your moment and the opportunity presents itself, you must be wholly present.

BRILLIANT DECREE

This is my moment. Power and potential are in it. I accept it and won't deny it. I welcome this moment and celebrate it, no matter what's in it. I will make my moment count because today might just be the moment that I have been waiting for. There will be times that I will like it and times when I won't, but it is still my moment, and I choose to occupy it.

BRILLIANT
NEXT STEP

Today, I want you to do something bold and out of the norm for you. Drive home a different way. Go out to dinner in the middle of the week rather than waiting for the weekend.

INSIGHT 31
FIVE WAYS TO FINISH BRILLIANTLY

(Mental)

Here are five of my favorite insights that will empower you to finish everything you do on a high note:

1. Be big, think big, and act big.

Benjamin E. Mays, former president of Morehouse College, once said, "The tragedy of life is often not in our failure, but rather in our complacency; not in our doing too much, but rather in our doing too little; not in our living above our ability, but rather in our living below our capacities." What can you do to drive value in all that you do? Make it happen.

2. Be open to happy accidents.

Joe Jaworski, author of *Synchronicity: The Inner Path of Leadership*, says, "Serendipity is when you go to a place, a setting, or a meeting expecting a certain outcome and discover something entirely different because you are open and are present to the moment."

In "Perceptions of Serendipity," published in the *Journal of Counseling Psychology*, we learn that "career analysts find that 83% of midcareer professionals believe chance (serendipity) played a significant role in their ultimate career path and that they highly value staying open for unexpected opportunities."

Keep moving forward. You never know what you might bump into, my friend.

3. Be intentional with your time and energy.

Vilfredo Pareto was an Italian economist who in 1906 observed that 20 percent of the Italian people owned 80 percent of their country's accumulated wealth. Now to put this into context: Eighty percent of your success is the result of 20 percent of your efforts. Determine how you can move the needle by becoming laser-like in your daily efforts, rather than being a floor lamp that diffuses its energy, or a strobe light that can't focus on any one thing.

4. Be desperate.

In his latest book, *David and Goliath* (a must-read), Malcolm Gladwell shares an amazing story about University of Louisville basketball coach Rick Pitino: "In 1978, when he was twenty-five years old, Pitino used the full court press to take the school to its first NCAA tournament appearance in twenty-four years. Pitino says he has many coaches come to Louisville every year to learn the press. They turn around and e-mail him and tell him that they can't do it. He tells them, 'We practice every day for two hours. The players are moving almost ninety-eight percent of the practice. We spend very little time talking.'"

The coaches who came to learn from Rick Pitino *were not desperate* enough to change. Gladwell makes the point that to beat the Goliath in your life, you have to be desperate enough to do the unconventional.

5. Be a Storyteller.

Contagious, by Jonah Berger is one of my favorite books. He says, "People don't share information; they tell stories. But just like the epic tale of the Trojan horse, stories are vessels that carry things such, as morals and lessons. Information travels under the guise of what seems like idle chatter. So we need to build our own Trojan horses, *embedding* our products and ideas in stories that people want to tell. Make your message so integral to the narrative that people can't tell the story without it."

When a person decides to finish brilliantly, they heed the advice of the late Robin Williams when he says in the movie *Dead Poets Society*: "Carpe diem. Seize the day, boys. Make your lives extraordinary."

BRILLIANT DECREE

Today I choose to finish what I start. I will align my head, my heart, and my hands to create a life of significance. I am brilliant.

BRILLIANT
NEXT STEP

Expand your mind. You are the sum total of the 60,000 thoughts per day that have passed through your mind since you were a child.

Expand your thinking by writing down what is right and true about you and the difference your life will make. Meditate on this list, and review it every day.

Shift Your Brilliance

HARNESS THE POWER OF YOU, INC.

Experience the Brilliance Community at
www.simontbailey.com

Why Shift & Why Now?

Shift Your Brilliance

The phrases "shift your brilliance" and "vujá dé" will be used somewhat interchangeably throughout this book, but each plays a slightly different role in the production of your life. To give credit where credit is due, it was actually the late comedian George Carlin who coined the phrase "vujá dé" (pronounced voo-ja day). To him it meant the opposite of déjà vu, which according to Dictionary.com is "the illusion of having previously experienced something actually being encountered for the first time," or "disagreeable familiarity or sameness." A vujá dé moment is when you see everything as if for the first time, or better still, you see everything everyone else sees, but you understand it differently, more keenly. So what does it mean to shift your brilliance? The "shift" is simply putting into action the awareness that you need to focus your energy in new, different directions—it's that inner signal of change on the horizon and having the capacity to facilitate that change through your brilliant ideas, unique contributions, and futuristic thinking.

My Personal Shift Story

I have a confession to make. It was getting pretty easy for me to dispense advice—to put my finger on the pulse of the marketplace and make declarations about problems and solutions. And it has always been second nature for me to encourage other people to live meaningful lives and to become their most brilliant selves.

Since leaving my job as Sales Director of Disney Institute at the Happiest Place on Earth—Walt Disney World—to launch the Brilliance Institute, Inc., I had been on a roll. In less than seven years, *Meetings and Conventions* magazine had cited me as one of the top keynote speakers ever heard or used. This put me in the same category with Bill Gates, Colin Powell, and Tony Robbins.

The Society of Human Resource Management asked me to be a backup speaker to Lance Armstrong in case his private plane didn't make it to Las Vegas in time for the opening general session; the society just mentioned in passing that it would have 15,000 leaders from 70 countries. I didn't even break a sweat. I said to myself, "Bring it on, Baby." Well, as fate would have it, he did show up, but it was sure nice to be wanted (even as a backup).

After 13 rejection letters from major book publishers, I had also finally sold the rights to my book *Release Your Brilliance* to Harper-Collins, and they published it in hardcover. It went on to become seventeenth out of the top 100 books being read by Corporate America, according to 800-CEO-READ. Currently it is available in English, Spanish, and Portuguese and will soon be available in other languages.

After seven magical years and four different jobs at Disney and then my own consulting business with 300 different organizations from Fortune 500 companies, educational institutions, and government agencies in less than eight years, I realized I'd learned some valuable lessons and enjoyed some great success.

What I didn't realize at the time, though, was that my work was suddenly becoming mechanical, as if I were running on cruise control. In fact, I realize now that my heart was yearning for something else. It was trying to get me to go in a different direction. But business was good, and my head and my hands kept me doing the same things I'd been doing. They suspended me in a comfort zone; they refused to stretch beyond it.

The truth is that I was holding on to what had worked yesterday, thinking it would carry me into tomorrow. I was driving a Delta 88 in a Tesla world. But as fate would have it, something intervened—something interrupted my pleasant reverie and shook me to my very core.

It was around the time Barack Obama was elected President of the United States, and our already reeling economy was getting even worse. I looked with horror at my future bookings for speaking engagements and saw that for a solid 30-day period, there were none. The calendar was empty! And there were only drips of business in the coming months.

How could this be happening? The truth was hard to accept: My business was surviving on life support, holding on by a thread, and for the first time in my career, I felt a surge of panic. Up until that moment, everything I had done had worked for me. Suddenly, I went from confidence—bolstering and cheering on others—to feeling anything but optimistic. I, who had always rebuked and flagrantly dared pessimism to come my way, felt suddenly and severely dejected.

Finding myself in this state, I turned instinctively to prayer and time on the sideline to search for answers. I crossed and uncrossed my fingers a lot. I found myself opening and shutting the refrigerator door even more. Yet it wasn't food I was hungry for. My stomach wasn't what was empty; it was my soul. I was literally stuck in neutral, going nowhere fast. I knew I needed a major shift in my thinking and doing. How could I inspire brilliance in others if I lacked that clarity and passion for myself?

About that time, I connected with a client who was planning to host a business meeting for Merck-Serono Pharmaceuticals in Paris. They booked me to speak at the conference and I accepted. The presentation topic was "How to Release Your Brilliance."

As I packed for the trip and made the journey across the Atlantic, I realized it had been ten years since I had last been to Paris. It was on that previous trip, at age 30 and with Disney, while standing underneath the Eiffel Tower that I had reflected on the words of Dick Nunis (former chairman of Walt Disney Attractions). He said, "The higher you go, the less you know." I realized in that instant that I had gone as far as I could go at Disney, even though at one time I had said I wanted to be the Chairman and CEO one day.

I decided to do the unthinkable—leave my wonderful job at Walt Disney World and start my own consulting and speaking business. As good as the Disney organization had been for and to me, I realized that it was time to move on to the next stage in my life. It was my vujá dé moment.

Something about that sky-piercing, elegant Parisian architectural icon had vitalized me. It was a profound moment. Something truly monumental happened to me that day, and I knew I'd never be the same. I decided to ascend the staircase of the Eiffel Tower instead of taking the elevator lift. The higher I went, the more challenging it became. It was in this moment that I realized I was climbing the stairs because I knew in my heart that I belonged at the top of anything and everything I did. It was as if there were an internal click, a voice directing me to move, and I had finally discovered my purpose. For a brief moment I saw into my own crystal ball of choice.

When I returned home, my wife and I discussed what my next move would be. I'll never forget what she said: "No matter what, I am with you." Wow! That was the vote of confidence I needed. It was what gave me the courage to turn down four job offers in a 90-day period—offers that would have been easier to take rather than risking it all to follow my heart and what seemed like a calling.

My wife's unwavering dedication, my strong faith, and the memory of the elegant and inspiring tower created the momentum that allowed me to shift and set off into the unknown. There were no guarantees and no backup plan. This had to work.

Now a decade later, it was with both excitement and a bit of apprehension that I set out for my second trip to the City of Light. I had a feeling that, once again, things weren't going to be the same when I returned.

As I walked along the Champs-Elysees and into the nearby neighborhoods, the first thing I noticed was what a difference time makes. I'd endured a lot of change, both good and bad. My hair had grayed a bit, and I had begun to see my friends and family members pass away, reminding me just how precious life is. I no longer fought to hold back tears; now comfortable with my emotions in a way I hadn't been ten years earlier. It had taken me 40 years to get to this point, but I realized that I was free—liberated from the limitations of my past, from living a life just to please other people, and free to believe in and choose my own values. Free to *vujá dé*—to live my future now.

Standing before the Eiffel Tower once again, I listened for the voice I had so distinctly heard ten years before, and to my astonishment, I believe I really did hear something. It was a small but insistent voice, and it was repeating the same message I'd been receiving both in my heart and head for the past 18 months.

This time, the voice was very clear. It was telling me to *shift*.

I knew I had to get involved in my work in a deeper way. I had to make a deeper commitment. I knew that when I returned to the States, I needed to pour more into my writing; make it more substantive, direct, crisp. I needed to reveal my truths more honestly. I wanted to forge more profound, authentic connections with my clients and readers.

After several months of staying true to this new goal, I can honestly say it has made a huge difference in my life and my work. While I was already receiving positive responses to my monthly e-newsletter that goes out to thousands of people, it was little compared to now. People used to tell me that my words had inspired them, but nothing like they are telling me now.

By finding my courage and support in others, looking at things in a new way, and crystallizing a vision to take me to new levels of meaning and success, I was able to ignite my passion and shift. Here are some questions to consider:

- What could a personal shift do for you?

- Are you holding on to what worked yesterday?

- Are you suppressing your inner voice that is telling you to step out of your comfort zone?

- What mysterious voice or vision are you ignoring?

- Can you immerse yourself in your work or in your relationships in a more significant way?

Read this book as the first step to finding the power and inspiration to SHIFT! While *vujá de* is the what, *shifting your brilliance* is the how.

Brilliant Shifts All Around Us

A modern-day example of a business that employs a shift of brilliant thinking is a relatively new company called Uber.

With the creation of its downloadable apps, Uber is "evolving the way the world moves," through connecting taxi and private car riders with drivers at the touch of a button. The company has launched in over 35 cities and has globally disrupted the taxi and private car space, and in turn, has shifted how we arrange transportation. CEO and Co-Founder Travis Kalanick states on the website, "Every problem has a solution. You just have to be creative enough to find it." Only this kind of shift in brilliance can propel a company from a niche market in one city to a global presence less than five years later.

Cirque du Soleil is another example. If you've been to one of their performances, you know it's the circus on steroids— prescribed ones. Using a fresh set of eyes, they shifted what we normally thought of as a circus in a profound way. How many times do people leave a regular circus show and rave about how great it was? Very rarely, I bet. Why? There is no shift of brilliance.

There are many ways to shift your brilliance. Start by looking for the uncommon in the common, for meaning behind the actions and the words, for the new in the old. Like the entrepreneurs at Uber and Cirque du Soleil, you too, can discover innovative and breakthrough solutions. And, I promise you don't have to have really cool apps or a flying trapeze.